SEEING DOUBLE

SEEING

Over 200 Mind-Bending Illusions

DOUBLE

J. RICHARD BLOCK

Routledge
Taylor & Francis Group

NEW YORK AND LONDON

Joe Miranda, Editor
Paul Johnson, Editorial Assistant
Ben McCanna, Project Manager

Design and typography by Shelley Himmelstein.
This book was composed in Latin 725, Latin Extra Condensed, ITC Franklin Gothic,
Bank Gothic, AT Sackers Gothic, and Coronet Bold.

Cover design by Jennifer Crisp.
Cover art: "Ambiguous Cube: Wood," by Tony Azevedo.
Back cover art: (*Top*) "Three-stick Clevis," by D. H. Shuster; (*bottom*) "Magic Head,"
from *Upside-Down Heads* (Redstone Press, 1998).

Prepress by Jay's Publishers Services.
Printed on Somerset Matte by RR Donnelley & Sons Company, Willard.

Published in 2002 by
Routledge
29 West 35th Street
New York, New York 10001
www.routledge-ny.com

Published in Great Britain by
Routledge
11 New Fetter Lane
London EC4P 4EE
www.routledge.co.uk

Routledge is an imprint of the Taylor & Francis Group.

10 9 8 7 6 5 4 3 2 1

Library of Congress Cataloging-in-Publication Data

Block, J. R.
       Seeing double : over 200 mind-bending illusions / J. Richard Block.
           p. cm.
Includes bibliographical references and index.
       ISBN 0-415-93482-6 (pbk. : alk. paper)
   1. Optical illusions—Pictorial works. I. Title.
       QP495 .B563 2002
       152.14'8—dc21

                                                    2002009235

To my wife, Patricia, who treats me twice as well as she should.

CONTENTS

INTRODUCTION

Seeing Double is a collection of over 200 illustrations, each of which can be seen as having at least two different meanings or representations—but—not at the same time! These illustrations have been developed by psychologists, graphic artists, and fine artists. Some are centuries old, while many others are contemporary.

Several different methods have been used to produce these figures. The chapters of *Seeing Double* are roughly organized according to these methods, although one could argue that in some cases a particular figure should be included in a different chapter. Some of the "different" chapters are largely variations on other chapters.

A "Figure-Ground Illusion" (so called by psychologists) is one way to produce more than one conceptual image from a single image. While there are exceptions, when we look at an image, the figure we see is usually darker than its background; has a more clearly defined shape; and is smaller than the material on which it is presented. The chapter on figure-ground relationships presents images where these three characteristics are much more evenly balanced than is usually the case. If the size and shape of the light and dark areas are balanced, two different images can be seen. When this happens, it qualifies for inclusion in *Seeing Double.* You can see each of the different black-and-white images, but you cannot focus on one to the exclusion of the other!

The next set of illustrations, "Ambiguous Figures," consists of cases where a single image can be perceived in two or more ways. Here, the artists have used the shape of a given line to serve two different functions, depending on your "perceptual set," i.e., what you expect to see. Thus, if one were to design an ambiguous figure intended to show two different faces, the curve of a line could be used to represent the chin of one face and—at the same time—the nose of another. In these figures, once you perceive the overall impression of one image, you automatically interpret a curve as a chin or a nose depending on which fits your perceptual set best at the moment. The line is simply a nose at one time, and a chin at another, and the change doesn't bother you at all! Perhaps just as interestingly, once you see both interpretations, it is impossible to remain focused on just one. The other will keep popping into your consciousness. It is for this reason that ambiguous figures are sometimes called "reversible figures."

Another set of images is called "Embedded Figures." In this case, the artist presents a single major figure. You know what it is. Often it is someone's face. However, on closer inspection you find that the face is composed of a great many different, smaller images, usually belonging to the same category—e.g., bodies of other people, fruits and vegetables, or animals. If you look at the major figure, you are able to ignore its component parts. However, if you look at the parts, you no longer see the major figure.

Other sets of images require you to turn the book in various directions to see the alternate meanings. Most of these involve turning the book upside down, but to see some of them you will have to turn the book clockwise or counterclockwise by 90 degrees or so. Others require your holding the book at eye level and tipping it away from you. The psychologists and artists who developed these illustrations have managed to create two different images. In many of the upside-down examples in this section of the book, there are two different faces, depending on which view you choose. Thus, the mouth of one may appear on the forehead of the other. However, you conveniently ignore this, and a completely different face appears when you look at it upside down. In this section, we have also incorporated a number of words that can be read either right side up or upside down. They are called "ambigrams." In these cases, most of the words are read as the same word from either perspective. As in the case of a mouth that appears on a forehead, when the letter "i" appears in an ambigram, the dot under the inverted "i"—which changes into another letter upside down—is simply ignored when we read it.

Finally, there are other images in *Seeing Double* that meet the criteria of being a single image which can be seen as at least two different things, yet are not based on any of the principles above. Here we present some very different principles, and each will be described when you reach the last chapter.

Some of the illusions are more difficult to see than others, and some people may not be able to see some of them at all. There are individual differences in our perceptual responses. They are not related to intelligence or any personality factor. *Seeing Double* is not intended to be a comprehensive or scientific exploration of illusions and visual oddities. It is simply for the enjoyment and recognition of the incredible flexibility of the human mind! Indeed, to emphasize this, we often include minor variations on the same thing, to show how different people approach the same matter from a slightly different perspective.

The goal of the book is that almost every page will make you:

    a) smile, or,

    b) say to yourself: "Isn't that clever," or,

    c) say to yourself: "Isn't that interesting," or, in the best of all worlds,

    d) all of the above!

We hope you enjoy the book, and we hope you enjoy sharing it with your friends.

CHAPTER 1

FIGURE-GROUND IMAGES

When we look at a figure, it is usually darker and smaller than its background and has a more precisely defined form. However, it is possible to balance these characteristics more carefully than is usually the case. If you focus on the dark spaces, as we usually do when looking at an image on a sheet of paper, you will see just one figure. Yet if you think of the dark areas as the background of a white figure, you see something quite different.

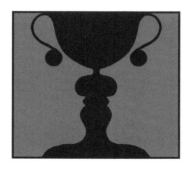

We open this chapter with a very well-known figure called "All Is Vanity." It shows a woman sitting at a vanity table and looking in a mirror. However, the back of her head and her reflected image are just the right distance apart—and the right size in the mirror—that they can be seen as the eyes of a skull. The items on the table make up the skull's teeth. While the image is well known, the artist, Charles E. Gilbert (1893–1929), is rarely credited. He was an American magazine illustrator, but during World War I he performed valuable work in ship camouflage and designed Liberty Loan posters.

The date of "All Is Vanity" is not known, but the present author believes it was the earliest of its type, and, as can be seen in the next few pages, it has been imitated many times. Many of the artists who produced these pictures are not known. Their works differ from Gilbert's in that they all use two heads to form the eyes of a skull or a man's face, while he used a reflected image.

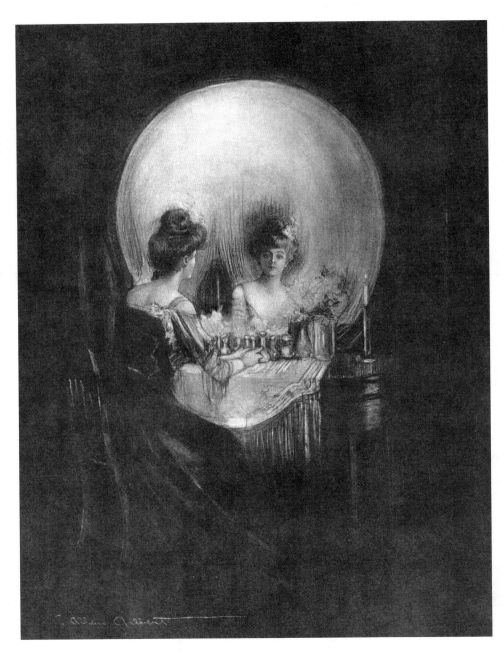

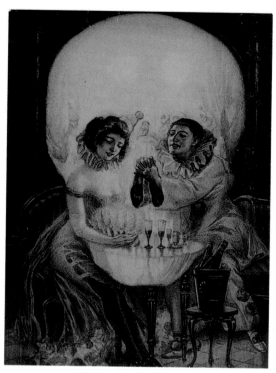

"L'Amour de Pierrot"
From the collection of Keith Kay.

From the collection of Keith Kay.

From the collection of Keith Kay.

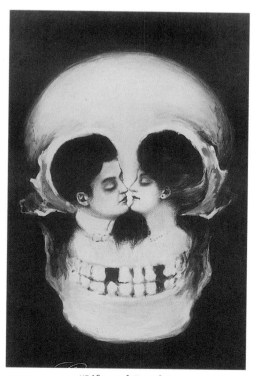

"Life and Death"
From The Playful Eye, *edited by Julian Rothenstein and
Mel Gooding, Redstone Press, 1999.*

Most of these images show couples, but one, by an artist named Callieni, called "Life and Death as Seen from Far and Near," shows two little girls playing with a dog.

The final image in this set is slightly different in that it shows two women who appear to be having a conversation, but the background—when viewed as the figure—becomes the face of the Devil. This drawing is called "Gossip, and Satan Came Also." It was made in the early 1900s by George A. Witherspoon, an American illustrator.

The theme of faces forming a skull has been used for political and social commentary when presented in a somewhat more elaborate form. The first example here is the cover of a U.S. magazine called *Judge,* published in May 1894. It was anti-tariff bill propaganda.

"Life and Death as Seen from Far and Near"
© 2002, The Puzzle Museum, Hordern-Dalgety Collection.
http://www.puzzlemuseum.com

"Gossip, and Satan Came Also"

From The Playful Eye, *edited by Julian Rothenstein and Mel Gooding, Redstone Press, 1999.*

A second example is a French postcard from 1906. It depicts the Russian imperial family at the time of a suppressed revolution in Russia (Rothenstein and Gooding, 1999).

The final illusion in this set is an early-twentieth-century lithograph from the United Kingdom, which is called "The 'Unspeakable' Turk: An Arch and Foul (Fowl?) Mystery."

© *Bodleian Library, University of Oxford, John Johnson Collection, Puzzle Pictures folder.*

We shift now to a series of much simpler figure-ground illustrations. The first few all show profiles of two faces if you focus on them, but a different object if you focus on the area that separates them. The earliest known example is called "Rubin's Vase," which was first presented by the Danish psychologist Edgar Rubin in 1921. We have included a second drawing of a goblet separating the faces.

"Rubin's Vase"

From the collection of Keith Kay.

These and similar illustrations probably inspired the Kaiser Porcelain company to produce a vase for the Silver Jubilee celebration of Queen Elizabeth and Prince Philip, on which representations of their profiles can actually be seen if the vase is placed against a dark background.

© Porzellan Manufaktur Staffelstein GmbH & Co. KG.

The next several images use an apple core, a flower, a candle, and a mosque to create the same effect.

A final example of two profiles involved in a figure-ground illustration can be found in the Canadian

From the collection of Keith Kay.

flag. If you focus on the red figure, it is the Canadian flag, with the national symbol of the maple leaf. However, if you focus on the white outline of the top half of the leaf as if *this* is the figure, with the red area as background, you can see the faces of two men whose foreheads touch. They have sharp long noses and open mouths, and appear to be shouting at each other. In Canada, they are sometimes known as Jack and Jacques, who may be arguing over the merits of English versus those of French!

Returning to some simple graphics, we can shift from seeing three white sailboats to green palm trees in the first example. Two sets of kitchen utensils are presented in the next example. One is white and the other brown. In the next figure, the white half of the image can be seen as a face in profile, while the blue half can be a beggar holding out his hand. In the fourth example, two glasses form the shape of a single bottle.

From the collection of Keith Kay.

These two examples show simple red or white, or green or white arrows, depending on which you choose as the figure.

Another example of a woman's face in a figure-ground image can be seen in a 1913 postcard published by J.M. Flagg in the United Kingdom, as part of a series called *Pictorial Comedy*. Most of the black figure can be seen as a map showing Africa, Europe, Asia, and Australia in the lower right. However, by adding the suggestion of an eye, nose, and mouth, Africa, Europe, and Asia become her hair.

CHAPTER 2

AMBIGUOUS FIGURES

The images in this chapter are called "ambiguous figures." In some respects they are similar to the figure-ground illusions in the last chapter, but ambiguous figures depend more on shared contours that take on different meanings, rather than on which of two images is considered the figure and which is the background at any given moment.

Research has shown that when there is a figure that can have two different meanings—as in the case of ambiguous figures—if one does not know that two interpretations are possible, the figure is usually perceived as having only one. However, once it is known that there are actually two figures in one, the figures often "reverse" themselves in an involuntary and automatic way, and, as we noted earlier, ambiguous figures are often called "reversible figures" (Rock, Hall, and Davis, 1994). We will start with some simple examples and proceed to much more sophisticated ones. Most people can see the two (or sometimes more) figures without help, but we will provide hints to help you see each of the images in the figure.

A good place to start is with a classic—if not *the* classic—ambiguous figure. It was first published in the U.K. magazine *Puck* (1915) by W.E. Hill, who called it "My Wife and My Mother-in-Law." This updated col-

"My Wife and My Mother-in-Law"

orized version contains the images of both a young woman and an old woman. As a hint, the chin of the young woman is the tip of the nose of the old woman. The short horizontal black line between the two dark masses at the bottom of the figure can be seen either as the mouth of the old woman or the necklace of the young woman.

Hill's drawing may have been inspired by earlier versions of this illusion. A similar image, created in the late 1880s, appeared on an advertising postcard for a company called Phenyo-Caffein Co., of Worcester, Massachusetts. This one is called "My Girl & Her Mother." While the image does not relate in any way to the Massachusetts company's products, one can only guess that they felt that the image was so interesting that the card would not be discarded and thus their commercial message would have added life.

"My Girl & Her Mother"

Not to be sexist, we include a more contemporary figure called "Husband and Father-in-Law" (Botwinick, 1961). Again, the horizontal line just below the middle of the figure can either be seen as the mouth of the old man or a neckband for the young man. The tip of the nose of the old man is the chin of the young man, who is turned slightly away.

But if you can get two faces from one, why not three? In 1968, Professor G.H. Fisher published "Mother, Father, and Daughter-in-Law." Near the middle of the figure is a small dark spot, which serves as the eye of the father, who faces right. He has a large moustache at the bottom of the figure. His eye also serves as the mother's eye. She faces left. She has a short, thin-lipped mouth and a large nose. The tip of her nose is the daughter's chin. The daughter also faces left and has a very small nose, the top of which is missing (Fisher, 1968b).

Fisher went even further in including multiple faces in a single image. The clown figure has seven faces. First, of course, there is the full one facing directly at you. Then there are two more facing left and right, with red noses. However, there are four more who face inward. Two of them are fairly large, with broad smiles close to the mouth of the full-faced clown. But just above them, there are two other faces

From the American Journal of Psychology. © *1961 by the Board of Trustees of the University of Illinois. Reprinted by permission of the University of Illinois Press.*

with short lips that look almost like commas on either side of the nose of the full-faced clown (Fisher, 1967a).

Another popular ambiguous figure from the early-twentieth century shows the head of an American Indian as well as an Inuit man looking out of an igloo into a storm. The American Indian faces left and his nose is the left elbow of the Inuit man. The dark area on the right is either a headdress or the storm outside the igloo.

A number of other simple ambiguous figures come from Dr. Fisher's work. First we present either a fist or a person wrapped in a blanket (Fisher, 1968a).

From the American Journal of Psychology. © *1967 by the Board of Trustees of the University of Illinois. Reprinted by permission of the University of Illinois Press.*

From the American Journal of Psychology. © *1968 by the Board of Trustees of the University of Illinois. Reprinted by permission of the University of Illinois Press.*

The figures in the next series all come from Fisher's 1968b article. First, we have a man's face or a woman holding a baby. Hint: The woman's face is the man's partially closed eye, and the baby is his ear. Next there is either a seated woman with her head turned away from you, or a man's face. The woman's right arm is the man's nose. Then we have a mermaid or a woman wearing a scarf. The mermaid has her back turned and her right arm is the woman's nose. Her tail flippers are the woman's scarf. The next image is either a rabbit or the head of an American Indian. The rabbit's ears form the headdress.

Perhaps a more difficult image to see is the mouse/boy figure. The boy is facing right. The dark area

From the American Journal of Psychology. © *1968 by the Board of Trustees of the University of Illinois.*
Reprinted by permission of the University of Illinois Press.

near the middle is the right eye of the boy who is seen in profile. It also serves as the mouse's right eye. The mouse's face is at the bottom of the figure (Fisher, 1968a).

The turkey/Inuit man might also give you some difficulty. The turkey's tail feathers become the Inuit man's face, while his right arm becomes the turkey's head (Fisher, 1968a). Fisher also produced the lion/flower figure, in which the lion's face is the center of the flower bud and his arm is the flower stem; and the seashell/elephant head figure, where the elephant's trunk points to the left and the mouth of the seashell is the elephant's ear (Fisher, 1968a).

From the American Journal of Psychology. © 1967, 1968 by the Board of Trustees of the University of Illinois. Reprinted by permission of the University of Illinois Press.

In the figure on the upper left, the head of a donkey becomes the full body of a seal. The donkey's ears become the seal's tail; its nostrils and mouth become the seal's head. In the angel/parrot figure, the parrot's beak becomes the angel's face (Fisher, 1968a). The charmed snake of the lower-left figure is alternately the screw of a corkscrew, and the snake's basket is the grip. The figure on the lower right can be seen either as a rat or a man's face (Bugelski and Amalpay, 1961). If you see a man's face, the two circles on the left are his eyes or eyeglasses. They become the mouse's ears, with the mouse's tail becoming the man's chin.

Upper-left and upper-right figures are from the American Journal of Psychology. © *1967, 1968 by the Board of Trustees of the University of Illinois. Reprinted by permission of the University of Illinois Press.*

The next figure is geometric. In some respects it is unusual, in that the figure we perceive is not actually printed on the page, but is formed by the green areas. Such figures are called "illusory figures," because we complete them from other information on the page. The figure looks like a ship's wheel. Yet the wheel can be considered to be composed of a circle, a plus sign (+), and an "X." Since each of these has equally good form, when you try to focus on just one of them, the others will pop in and out of your consciousness (Bradley and Dumais, 1975).

© Nature.

Ambiguous figures can also be seen in images that have a three-dimensional quality. This figure, "Ambiguous Cube: Wood," by Iowa graphic artist Tony Azevedo, can be seen as a large cube of wood, but the corner closest to you has a smaller cube shape cut into it. However, it can also be seen as a small cube set inside three pieces of wood, with the small cube resting on the darkest of these surfaces. The lines that form the small cube are balanced so evenly against the larger figure that if you stare at the center, it will shift from an indentation in the large surface to a solid small cube itself. This change will take place spontaneously, and you cannot focus on only one of its two aspects.

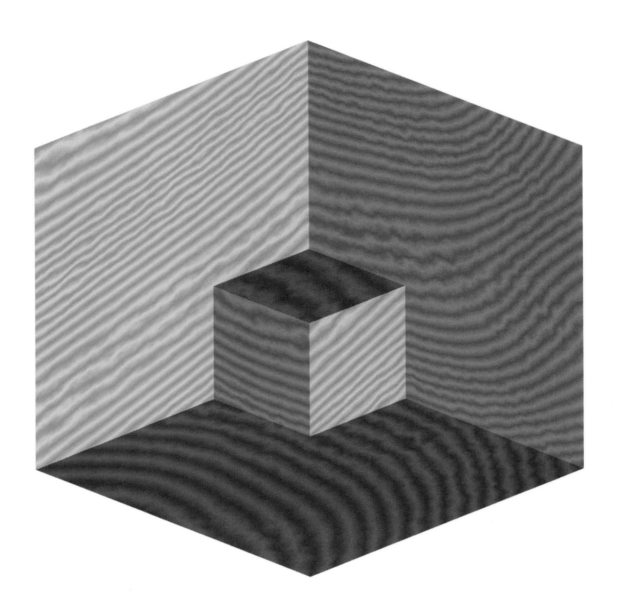

Before we go on to more sophisticated ambiguous images, we turn to two figures that take on quite different meanings depending on the context in which you perceive them. The figure in the center when looking right to left seems to be the letter "B," with "A" and "C" on either side. But this center figure is seen quite differently when you look at the numbers arranged vertically. In between 12 and 14, what was the letter "B" becomes 13.

Similarly, the figure that centers on the word "bicycle" when read right to left, is interpreted differently when we read the letters top to bottom as "ride." In one case the letters are "cl," and in the other they are seen as the letter "d."

However, these are very simple figures. There are more interesting and sophisticated images that have been developed by fine and graphic artists.

We will start with one from the early 1900s by George A. Witherspoon, titled "Society: A Portrait." You can see a finely dressed gentleman with top hat and dinner jacket, but you can also see the face of a donkey on his chest.

The next two examples are from the work of Paul Agule, a New York graphic artist. The first can either be seen as a shoe or a man's face, where the shoelaces are interpreted as glasses. In the second figure you can see a bespectacled man with a moustache and beard, or a weightlifter lifting a barbell.

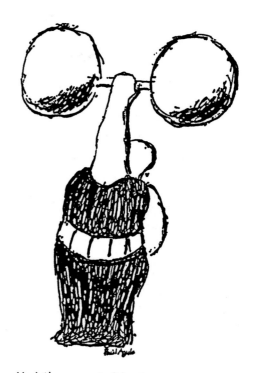

A barbell becomes a pair of glasses, etc.

Salvador Dalí, the internationally known Spanish surrealist painter, incorporated visual illusions into a number of his paintings. The first, presented here, is called "Paranoiac Figure." It can be seen as a face lying on its side in the sand, or as a group of seated figures looking off into the distance, with their backs facing you. It is said that this piece was inspired by a photograph Dalí had seen of an African village, which featured a group of villagers seated before their huts.

In 1939, Dalí painted "The Image Disappears." It can either be seen as the profile of a man with a beard and moustache, or a standing woman who appears to be reading.

In 1941, Dalí painted "The Mysterious Lip That Appeared on the Back of My Nurse." Here, one can see the seated figure of a woman looking off into the distance, with a child standing to her right. The woman's back forms the lower half of a person's face.

One of the most prolific artists to incorporate illusions into his work is Sandro Del Prete, a contemporary Swiss artist. In fact, he is so prolific that he and his wife have a museum and gallery devoted to optical illusions and holographic works, Illusoria Land, which is located in Ittigen/Bern, Switzerland. In addition to the examples of his work here and in a later chapter, other examples can be seen on the Internet at http://www.illusoria.com.

The first example of Del Prete's work included here is "Spirit of the Mountain." Like Dalí's work, "The Mysterious Lip That Appeared on the Back of My Nurse," this piece shows us the back of a woman seated on a mound of grass and looking into the distance. Her back forms the nose of the mountain man, with the grass and tree stump forming his beard and moustache.

Another of Del Prete's works is called "Homage to Leonardo da Vinci." In this figure one can see da Vinci's profile as he paints a rider on horseback. However, his facial features can also be seen as a second rider, identical to the one he is painting.

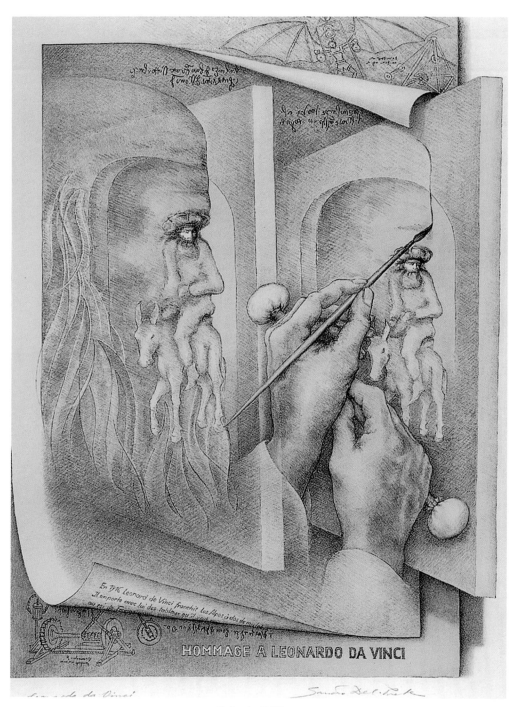

© Sandro Del Prete.

In "Window Gazing," we see a young boy and girl looking out of a window. The illusion comes about when we find that sometimes the window appears to be facing right, and then suddenly left! This is an example of what is called an "impossible figure." In other words, you could not construct such a window, but you can see it. We will see other impossible figures later in the book.

© Sandro Del Prete.

In Del Prete's "St. George and the Dragon," he presents us with a portrait of St. George at the center of the image, but the portrait can also be seen as St. George killing the dragon with his lance.

© Sandro Del Prete.

In "The Flowering of Love," one sees a single rose. However, the top center petals can also be seen as a couple kissing.

© *Sandro Del Prete.*

Another very prolific contemporary artist who includes illusions as central features in his works is Mexican-born Octavio Ocampo, who studied at the Art Institute of San Francisco. We present three of his ambiguous figures here and will see two other examples of his work in a later chapter.

In the first, called "Palm Sunday," we see a portrait of Jesus Christ, but we also see him entering Jerusalem on donkey, with many cloaked figures gathering around.

The second example of Ocampo's work, "Calvary," also has a religious theme. Here we also see the face of

© Octavio Ocampo. Courtesy of Amazing Art Images, LLC.

Jesus, but we see him on the cross. The painting also shows three eyes, which symbolize the Father, Son, and Holy Ghost. Ocampo has indicated that the rightmost eye represents the Holy Ghost encircled with doves symbolizing peace and love.

© Octavio Ocampo. Courtesy of Amazing Art Images, LLC.

The third example of Ocampo's work is called "Visions of Quixote." Ocampo has presented a portrait of Don Quixote of La Mancha, but you also see him with his lance, riding his faithful steed, Rocinante, with windmills in the background. The left eye of the large portrait is Don Quixote, with the right eye showing his trusted companion, Sancho Panza. The face of his beloved Dulcinea can be seen in the upper-left corner.

© Octavio Ocampo. Courtesy of Amazing Art Images, LLC.

Finally, in this chapter we will see variations on a theme, all of which present what appear to be both the top and bottom of a surface. These again are impossible figures. We cannot precisely date each of them, but we think that the first was what Del Prete called "Folded Chess Set," which he made in 1983. He creates the illusion that we can see the chessboard from below and above, but not at the same time.

Das gekrümmte Schachbrett

© *Sandro Del Prete.*

More recently, Tony Azevedo produced a similar figure he calls "Endless Chess." The opposing pieces can never actually confront each other on this board. His work appears on the Internet at http://www.SandlotScience.com, a site that is devoted to the presentation of visual illusions and related materials.

Another variation on this theme appears on a number of Web sites. It is variously called "Folded Terrace," "Strange Terrace," and "Impossible Patio."

CHAPTER 3

LEFT/RIGHT

The next set of figures really represents a subset of ambiguous figures. These differ only to the extent that seeing the two different images in each is largely a matter of focusing on the left or right side of the image, rather than focusing on either side of a shared contour. Most of these figures are quite simple.

The oldest in the set presented here was drawn by an American psychologist, Joseph Jastrow, in 1888. Focusing on the left, you see a duck, but focusing on the right, you see a rabbit.

Another old image shows the silhouette of a flying bird. If you see it flying to the left, it is a goose, but if it is flying to the right, it is a hawk. Similarly, the next figure is a pelican if you see it facing left, and a rabbit if facing right (Kay, 1988).

The psychologist G.H. Fisher, whose work we saw earlier, also developed the next three figures. The swan/squirrel figure also works this way. Viewed on the

From the collection of Keith Kay.

left, the image is a swan's head and neck, but the swan's tail feathers on the right become a squirrel's head. The next figure can be a goldfish if it is seen swimming to the upper right, while it is the face of a young woman with a scarf if the figure is facing left (Fisher, 1968a).

Similarly, the lower-left figure is a mouse or a hippopotamus. In the last of this set of left/right images, you can see two different girls, depending on whether you look at the left or right side of the figure.

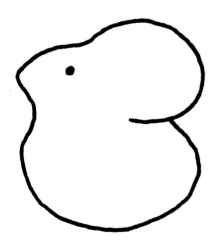

Upper-left and upper-right figures are from the American Journal of Psychology. © *1967, 1968 by the Board of Trustees of the University of Illinois. Reprinted by permission of the University of Illinois Press.*

The remaining images in this chapter come from another set of visual illusions we have described as "impossible figures." These are drawings of objects that appear to be solid, yet cannot be manufactured.

The first of these is called a "three-stick clevis" (Schuster, 1964). If you start at the left, you expect to see two bars as you move to the right, but by the time you get there, you find there are three!

In an article in *Scientific American,* Martin Gardner includes a drawing by Roger Haywood, who took the three-stick clevis and embellished it while turning it clockwise 90 degrees. The simple arms of the clevis have now become part of an ancient ruin. You do not view this left to right, but rather top to bottom. The ruin has two columns starting at the top, but there are three in the water (Gardner, 1970).

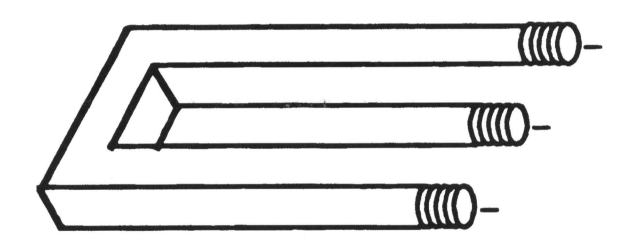

From Roger Hayward, in Mathematical Games, *by Martin Gardner, p. 124.*
© *1970 Scientific American. Reprinted by permission.*

The next figure is a strange rectangle. One can think of it as a rectangular window frame. On the left, the frame appears to be standing upright, but on the right, it is lying on its side (Draper, 1978).

The steps in the next figure are also impossible. If you started from the lower-left side you would have to climb four steps, but if you start at the upper right, you only have to climb one to get to the same level (Huffman, 1971).

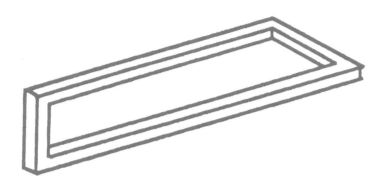

From Draper, S.W., (1978). The Penrose triangle and a family of related figures. Perception 7, pp. 283–296, London: Pion.

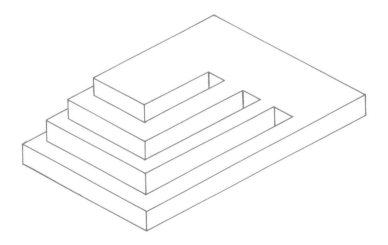

CHAPTER 4

EMBEDDED FIGURES

With "embedded figures," there is one main figure that is readily seen. In most of the examples in *Seeing Double*, the figure is a person's face. However, the face, or whatever the main figure may be, is composed of a large number of smaller figures. In most cases, these smaller figures all have characteristics that relate to each other and all relate in some way to the main figure. Very little explanation is required for you to enjoy this chapter. One can simply appreciate the artists' skill in arranging and shaping each of the small figures to fit into the primary figure in a meaningful way.

The "father" of embedded figures would have to be Giuseppe Arcimboldo. Indeed, we might call him the "great-great-grandfather," since he painted these complex figures in the sixteenth century. His style was unique at the time, but he has been imitated frequently since. In fact, one often refers to more recent works involving embedded figures as being "in the style of Arcimboldo" or "Arcimboldoesque." Arcimboldo served three emperors of the Habsburg dynasty, which ruled what is now Austria for over six centuries. He was appointed by Emperor Ferdinand I as Court Painter to the Vienna Imperial Court in 1562, and continued to

"Spring"
© *Réunion des Musées Nationaux / Art Resource, New York.*

EMBEDDED FIGURES

serve during the reigns of emperors Maximilian II and Rudolf II.

It is appropriate, then, that this chapter begins with examples of his work. The first four paintings are called "The Four Seasons." Each face is made up of vegetation consistent with the time of year. Thus, we have flowers, fruits and vegetables, turning leaves, and bare branches. The four seasons were painted in 1573, and indeed you can see the date woven into the shoulder of "Summer," with his name woven into the collar. The original paintings are in the Louvre Museum in Paris.

"Summer"
© *Réunion des Musées Nationaux / Art Resource, New York.*

"Fall"

© *Réunion des Musées Nationaux / Art Resource, New York.*

"Winter"
© *Réunion des Musées Nationaux / Art Resource, New York.*

We have another example of Arcimboldo's work in this chapter. It is called "The Librarian." The head and body of the figure are made up of books. This work, designed to please Maximilian II, was intended to be a portrait of the emperor's librarian, Wolfgang Lazius. It was painted in 1566. The original is in Skokloster Castle

Courtesy of LSH Foto.

in Skokloster, Sweden. Still another example of Arcimboldo's embedded figures is in the next chapter, because it has to be turned upside down to be seen.

Below is an anonymous drawing from the late-eighteenth-century called "Isle of Dogs," for obvious reasons.

The next two examples of embedded figures are Japanese woodblocks produced circa 1850. The first is called "A Kindly Man of Fearful Aspect." The artist was Utagawa Kuniyoshi. The Japanese call this form of embedded figure paintings *Yose-e* ("putting things together"). The Japanese text says: "I made a good person of many people. If you want to be a good person you must help others."

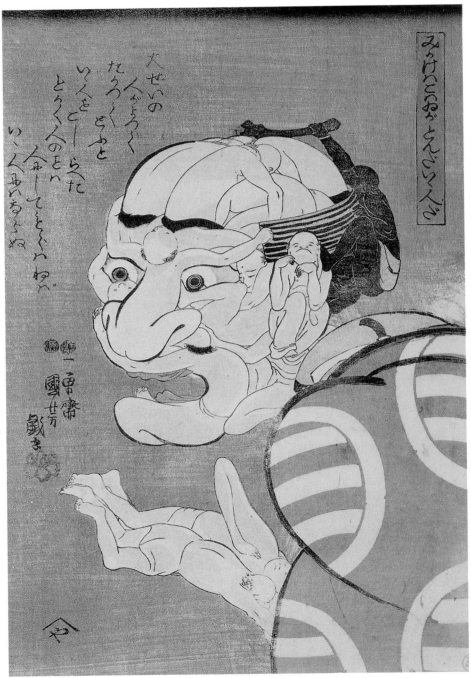

From The Paradox Box, *Redstone Press, 1993.*

The second woodblock is called "Cat and Kittens" (Rothenstein and Gooding, 1999). It was created by Ipposai Yoshifuji sometime between 1847 and 1852. He was one of the artists in the Utagawa school, and studied under the master printmaker Kuniyoshi. Both of them loved cats. The large cat's eye is a bell, and the whiskers are the ribs of a fan. There are eighteen kittens arranged to form the figure of the adult cat. The Utagawa school had a major influence on Western art.

Courtesy of Shin'ichi Inagaki.

The next two figures are portraits of Napoleon, drawn with embedded figures. The first was published in the United Kingdom by R. Ackermann in about 1810.

The caption on the original says that the hat represents the "maimed and crouching French Eagle," and the face is composed of "the corpses of the victims of his

© 2002, The Puzzle Museum, Hordern-Dalgety Collection.
http://www.puzzlemuseum.com

folly and ambition." Perhaps because it originates from France in the same era, the second portrait is more flattering, with military figures composing the head of Napoleon.

The next two figures are both representations of the devil. Both were drawn in about 1900. The first is called "Mephisto" and was done in the United Kingdom. The second is called "Diabolo," and was done in France.

"Mephisto"
© 2002, The Puzzle Museum, Hordern-Dalgety Collection.
http://www.puzzlemuseum.com

"Diabolo"
© 2002, The Puzzle Museum, Hordern-Dalgety Collection.
http://www.puzzlemuseum.com

Returning to the work of Octavio Ocampo, whose ambiguous faces we saw earlier, we see a figure he calls "The General's Family." One can see the profile of an elderly man with a beard and moustache, but we can also see that it is made up of several figures, including a man and a woman holding a baby, as well as a dog lying on its side, representing the General's hand. There are also nine heads hidden in the figure. For example, faces can be seen at either end of the arch above the main figure.

© Octavio Ocampo. Courtesy of Amazing Art Images, LLC.

The second example of Ocampo's work in this chapter is called "Forever Always." Ocampo uses the concept of two faces making a vase, as we saw in the chapter on figure-ground illusions, but embellishes it significantly. The face of the old woman on the left is made up of the full figure of a younger woman, and the face of the old man is made up of a young man. Ocampo has indicated that the couple sees each other as they were when they were much younger, when he courted her with serenades as they drank tequila with limes. The old man's ear is formed by the figure of a young woman, and Ocampo says that you can look into his mind to note that he always sees his wife as beautiful and desirable. He calls the cup in the center of the picture the "cup of love."

Next are two examples of embedded figures by Swiss artist Sandro Del Prete. The first is called "Einstein," with his face composed of three young women who are bathing. The second is called "The Invisible Neptune," with Neptune's body made up of fish, seaweed, and a sunken ship.

"Einstein"
© *Sandro Del Prete.*

"The Invisible Neptune"
© Sandro Del Prete.

Finally, we have an embedded figure painted by Salvador Dalí in 1936. It is called "The Great Paranoiac," and shows a face composed of what appear to be tormented people.

EMBEDDED FIGURES

CHAPTER 5

UPSIDE DOWN

In the next three chapters, you will have to move the book around to see the different images; in this chapter, you will have to turn the book upside down. We will begin with words or names called "ambigrams." Ambigrams are words that can be read from angles other than that at which the text is normally presented.

What better way to begin this chapter than with the words "upside down?" You will see that this image reads exactly the same way whether you hold the book as you normally would or turn it upside down. The presentation of these two words was designed by Scott Kim for his book, *Inversions* (Kim, 1989). You will note that, as we said in the Introduction, the fact that there is an "i" in "upside" that has the dot over it in one position, but underneath the word when inverted, does not seem to bother us at all. It is perfectly all right in its "proper" perspective, but is simply ignored when it is wrong in the upside-down version. The most important thing for us is to be able to organize most of the information on the page. In this first example, the word "upside" becomes a different word—"down"—when inverted.

© Scott Kim.

The remaining examples of Kim's ambigrams in this chapter are not totally true to the theme of *Seeing Double,* in that instead of seeing two different images from one, you actually see exactly the same image upside down and right side up. Thus, as noted, when we deal with the names of the three famous artists and encounter the letter "i" in "Stravinsky," we ignore the dot when it is below the word. Similarly, although the first down stroke in the letter "M" in Mozart has a cross in it so it can be seen as a "t" when it is inverted, we conveniently ignore the line when it is the first letter in the name (Kim, 1989).

Stravinsky

mozart

rembrandt

Mr. Kim does not limit his creativity to famous names. On this page you can see ambigrams of six fairly common first names. Further, if your first name—or your friend's name—is any of the following, you can find it inverted as an ambigram in *Inversions*: Annie, Chris, Daniel, Dave, Gordon, Gregg, Irene, Jill, Kim, Leon, Michael, Naomi, or Victoria.

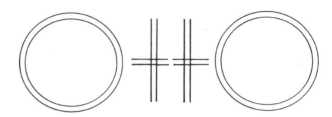

Before we proceed to more artistic representations of two different images when seen upside down, we present two photographs. Most of the time we see light coming from above us and creating shadows appropriate to the object it hits. Thus, in the first figure we see a crater formed by a meteor strike on Earth. The crater is Barrington Meteorite Crater, photographed here by D.J. Roddy and Z. Keeler of the United States Geological Survey office. We see a huge hole in the earth. When inverted, however, the shadowing makes it look like a large hill. The same effect is seen with large storage tank. It has rivets which bulge out and dents pressing inward. When viewed upside down the rivets appear to be going in, with dents bulging outward.

Using light and shadow, the graphic artist Tony Azevedo, whose work we saw earlier in "Ambiguous Figures," has created the image he calls "Figure Eight: Topsy Turvy." As you look at the image in the book, the number "8" appears on a wooden background, but it is made up of three pieces of a cork-like substance. The "8" itself is not actually there, but it is the space left out of what would be a solid circle of cork. It looks like a stencil image. However, if you turn the figure upside down you still see the "8," but it now appears to be a solid figure of wood resting in the center of a circle of cork. The difference is in how you interpret the shadows. We are used to light coming from above and defining the figure it hits. When you look at the "8" right side up, the light appears to create sharp lines below the cork figures. Upside down, the shadows seem softer and define the "8" differently.

It is interesting that you can maintain the image of the "8" as a solid figure you see when the book is inverted, even when you return to the original perspective. However, if you blink or look away for a second or two, the "indented 8" appears immediately. Your visual memory of the "solid 8" is not as strong as the visual stimulus of the actual patterns of light and dark. The reverse, however, is not true. When you hold the book upside down and see the "solid 8," you cannot change it back to a cutout image. We have far less visual experience with stencil figures than we have with solid ones, and we relate what we see to our past experience.

A somewhat more complex figure of a bird in a tree has been developed by Kelvin Fonville, the Creative Director of Publications for Hofstra University, the present author's alma mater. Like Azevedo's "8," the bird in the tree cannot be seen from one perspective, but becomes quite three-dimensional when upside down. It too can be held for a short time when presented as printed in the book, but it disappears after looking away for a few seconds.

In "Embedded Figures," we noted that Giuseppe Arcimboldo could be considered the father and even the great-great-grandfather of this form of double image. He can also be considered to have the same relationship to figures that appear different, but are meaningful when viewed upside down. The next figure in this chapter is by Arcimboldo. It is called "The Vegetable Gardener." Like his other work, it is an embedded figure. When looked at from one perspective, it appears to be a bowl of vegetables. However, when inverted, it is a face. The painting was done in 1590 and is probably the first of its kind, or certainly one of the first. The original is in the Museo Civico Ala Ponzone in Cremona, Italy.

Below is a much more recent upside-down embedded figure, though it is still well over one hundred years old. This illustration, from France in the late nineteenth century, shows clowns forming a pyramid, but when inverted shows a single clown's face that is made up of the acrobatic figures (Rothenstein and Gooding, 1999). Translation: "I count nine clowns here: Seven in the pyramid, and two assisting. . . . Now you try!"

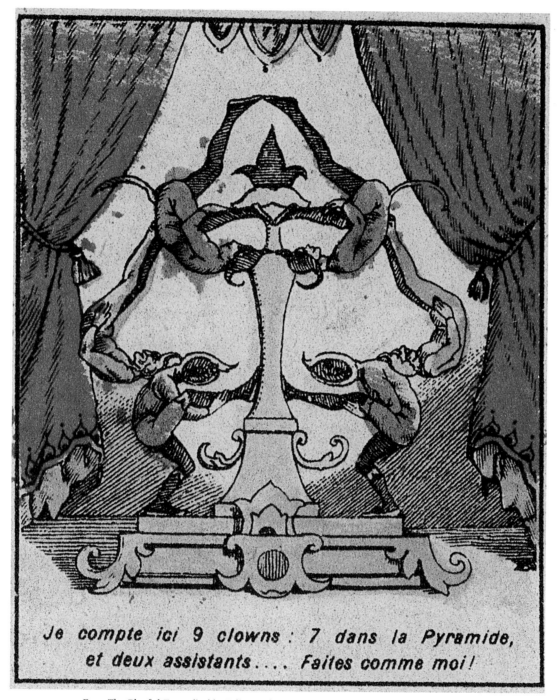

From The Playful Eye, *edited by Julian Rothenstein and Mel Gooding, Redstone Press, 1999.*

At about the same time in France, a deck of cards called *Jeu Grotesque* was published. In this deck, all of the aces, kings, queens, and jacks have the same general appearance. A single pair of eyes serves the full face in the center of each card with two profile faces on either side. The outermost faces appear as silhouettes.

When the card is inverted, five more faces can be seen. The playing cards themselves are in small boxes in the upper-left and lower-right corners. It is interesting that while this deck was published in about 1800, conventional playing cards did not use corner indices at that time.

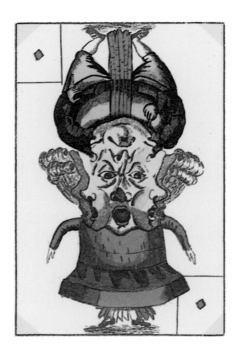

However, in about 1875, a card manufacturer in the United States named Andrew Dougherty began applying the same principle to cards he called "Triplicates." The center of the card was conventional, but there were the two small replicas in the corners. At about the same time, another U.S. playing card manufacturer, the Consolidated Card Company, published what we are now familiar with—the letters "A," "K,"

"Q," "J," or the number of the card with the suit symbol below. These cards were called "squeezers," and the numbers and suit symbols were quite small. Because they convey all of the necessary information more efficiently than small full-card replicas, they have become the standard, and we almost never look at the center of a playing card anymore.

1800

1875

1880

In terms of inverted images, faces have been a favorite subject over the years. Upside-down heads were very popular as illustrations on the covers of matchboxes and postcards, particularly in the late nineteenth century, although they continued to appear well after that. Here are several examples. The first six are from Spain. The first shows a military figure from one perspective and a horse from the other. The "Hussar" figure was done in 1860. "El Dragon" shows a military figure, but an elephant when viewed the other way. It is dated from 1870. The "Cossack," which also reveals a horse when turned upside down, was done in 1865.

"Hussar"

"El Dragon"

From Upside-Down Heads, *Redstone Press, 1998.*

"Cossack"
From Upside-Down Heads, *Redstone Press, 1998.*

Each of the following examples from Spain show a young woman from one view and a heavily bearded man from the other. Once again, we tend to ignore the nose and lips on the forehead. Both figures are dated 1875.

Es este hosco semblante,
al revés de buen talante,

Mi hermosura no sé alabe
vuelta, soy un Turco grave.

Translation:
My beauty is not praised in verse.
I'm a solemn Turk in reverse.

Here the face that wears a frown
is better looking upside down.

Si te enamoro bonito,
Sepas soy hermafrodito

Lo que es en mi vanidad,
vuelto, muestra gravedad.

Translation:
What seems to be my vanity
Turned upside down, appears as gravity.

If in your handsomeness I delight,
Know that I am a hermaphrodite.

From Upside-Down Heads, *Redstone Press, 1998.*

The third is from about the same time, but no date is available.

Translation:
So you see me, a pretty coquette,
And in reverse, I'm something else yet.

That which serves me to adorn,
What a shock! They are horns!

From The Paradox Box, *Redstone Press, 1993.*

The next inverted head is from Italy in 1946. It is a pamphlet cover from the Anti-Socialist/Communist Popular Front. It shows the face of Giuseppe Garibaldi from one view, but Joseph Stalin when turned upside down. The words read: "The Democratic Head? Turn it over and you will see the swindle." Garibaldi was an Italian hero who was a leader in the struggle for Italian unification and independence in the nineteenth century. Joseph Stalin was the communist head of state for the Union of Soviet Socialist Republics from 1924 until his death in 1953. It is not widely publicized, but Stalin changed his name in about 1913. His name was originally Dzhugashvili, but he changed it to Stalin because it means "man of steel."

The next two upside-down heads are from the United Kingdom. In the first, from 1850, we have a delightful bit of whimsy with an upside-down head.

Again, we conveniently ignore the eyes that appear at the chin of the figure that is right side up.

From Upside-Down Heads, *Redstone Press, 1998.*
© *Bodleian Library, University of Oxford: John Johnson Collection, Puzzle Pictures folder.*

In this image, "Sweethearts & Wives"—which was published in the United Kingdom in about 1890—we see five smiling faces from one view and five frowning faces from the other. It offers another example of how we ignore certain parts of our visual experience. When we look at a person's face at a relatively close range, we focus on the expressive features—the eyes and mouth. Here we see five faces and ignore the five mouths on the tops of their heads!

From Upside-Down Heads, *Redstone Press, 1998.*

This piece, also from the United Kingdom (circa 1880), was used as a visiting card. Here we have not a single face but a couple. The title is "Courtship and Matrimony," and the image shows two very different emotions on the two faces.

The upside-down matchbook cover from France circa 1900 says: "Search . . . and you will find the Basque peasant and the old Alsatian."

From Upside-Down Heads, *Redstone Press, 1998.*

The next figure is an eighteenth-century drawing showing a sinking ship. When viewed upside down you can see the captain's profile (Kay, 1997).

From the collection of Keith Kay.

During World War I, dozens of anti-German picture postcards were produced in England. Many of them incorporated portraits of Lord Kitchener, who was appointed Secretary of State for War by the British government in 1914. Lord Kitchener had a large handlebar moustache and was readily recognizable. Apart from his professional accomplishments, Lord Kitchener became quite famous in recruiting posters with his strong moustache, steely gaze, and pointed finger. One such recruiting poster is printed below. Next, a clergyman is shown when the image is viewed one way, and Lord Kitchener when turned upside down. Note the difference in the captions: where one reads, "Let Us Pray," the other reads, "Let Us Prey."

Kaiser Wilhelm II, emperor of Germany during World War I, also had a handlebar moustache, and the British enjoyed making fun of him. In the next example we see a caricature of the Kaiser appearing to be on the run. The original caption in this case read, "The British bulldog—puts the Germans on the run" (Kay, 1988). When the image is inverted, it shows the threatening bulldog. However, the fact that both of these strong personalities had similar moustaches must have made it almost irresistible to make them both parts of upside-down heads.

The next image here shows the Kaiser and Lord Kitchener together. Its original caption read, "To find the person who put the rope around the Kaiser's neck—turn the picture upside down," and we see Lord Kitchener once again (Kay, 1988).

The bottom two images maintain the same theme. In the first, the original caption said, "When German junkerism is completely overthrown, you will see Kitchener satisfied." The final image shows the Kaiser wearing a neckerchief. The original caption read, "The Kaiser and . . . Another reverse for him." There were many more variations, but these should give you some idea of what was popular at the time.

LET US PRAY

From the collection of Keith Kay.

The next three upside-down heads are from India. The military figures are from the late 1940s; the image featuring the woman's/man's faces (with glasses) was published circa 1970; the matchbook faces ("Magic Head") are from approximately 1940.

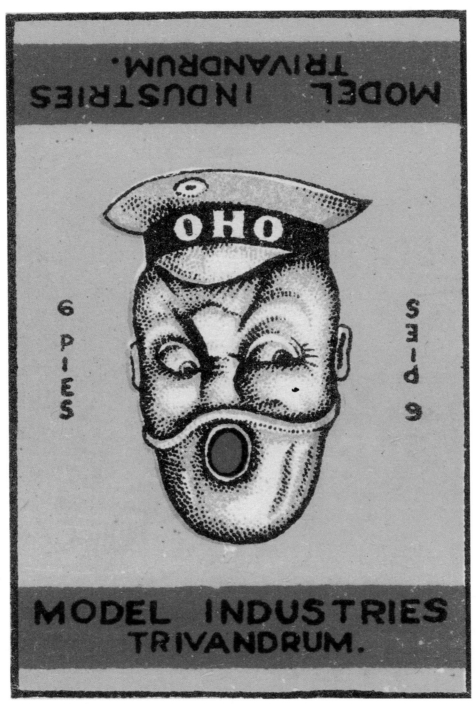

© 2002, The Puzzle Museum. Hordern-Dalgety Collection.
http://www.puzzlemuseum.com

From Upside-Down Heads, *Redstone Press, 1998.*

"Magic Head"
From Upside-Down Heads, *Redstone Press, 1998.*

Beginning in 1942 and continuing until about 1978, English artist Rex Whistler drew twenty-five upside-down pictures and his brother, Laurence, wrote poetry to go with each. They were published in a book called *AHA* in the United Kingdom in 1978. We present two here. On the left is the head of a young man from one perspective, which becomes the head of an old man when turned upside down. On the right, we have a portrait of Henry VIII from one view, and one of his fourth wife, Anne of Cleeves, from the other. King Henry married her in 1540 after seeing a portrait of her by German painter Hans Holbein. Holbein's portrait is much more flattering than Whistler's (Whistler, 1978).

"Young Man/Old Man"

"Henry and Anne"

The next image appears to show George and Martha Washington looking out the window at troops marching by. When inverted, a profile of George Washington can be seen (Kettelkamp, 1974).

Graphic artist Paul Agule, whose work we saw in "Ambiguous Figures," has produced the two charming upside-down images below. One shows a meerschaum pipe with smoke coming from the bowl, but when inverted, it looks very much like Santa Claus. The second appears to be a man sitting on a rock much like Rodin's sculpture, "The Thinker," but it is the face of an angry man when viewed the other way around.

and we have a bearded fellow in his stocking cap.

Paul Agule

Invert this meerschaum pipe...

ANGRY MAN

MAN SITTING ON A ROCK

Paul Agule

Over the years, a number of illustrators have put together storybooks for children using upside-down figures. One of the more recent examples is *The Amazing Topsy-Turvy Storybook* by Professor J.R. Calder of Heriot-Watt University in Scotland. Here we have the Three Musketeers from one perspective, but three old fishermen when viewed the other way (Calder, 1993).

Three old fishermen

Three old fishermen stroll by, with, in the background, sailing boats heading out to sea. The old men would be called 'old salts' - no doubt because fishermen get liberally sprayed with salt sea water during many years at sea.

The Three Musketeers

Here are three musketeers (the musket was an early form of rifle). The men are waving their hats in triumph, no doubt after a successful bout of sword-play.

At the end of the nineteenth century and into the early twentieth century, an American cartoonist by the name of Peter Newell published two books called *Topsys & Turvys*. Each image not only presents the basis for a story using both perspectives on the upside-down image, but the story is presented in verse. We offer a number of his stories here.

"Meow-meow! Pfitz-pfitz!—at me," says Mrs. Bulger's cat.

"Bow-wow! Wow-woof!" says Bulger's dog. What is he barking at?

His fine long-eared retriever plunged in and quickly got it.

A duck came flying o'er the pond; and when the sportsman shot it,

These little maids have been to town to purchase postage stamps,

And now are much alarmed to note their actions watched by tramps!

From Butterflies that flit about the meadows everywhere.

These Dames have modeled skilfully the gorgeous hats they wear,

But others claim this Duck was seen, and then the fact distorted.

Some say the famed Sea-serpent came, and by the shore disported,

And all the timid Dicky-birds are silent in the shade.

Some Indians in war-paint come tiptoeing through the glade,

But found the little manikin could well defend himself.

A wicked robber horseman charged upon a woodland elf,

The Ostrich has a longer neck and smaller mouth than his.

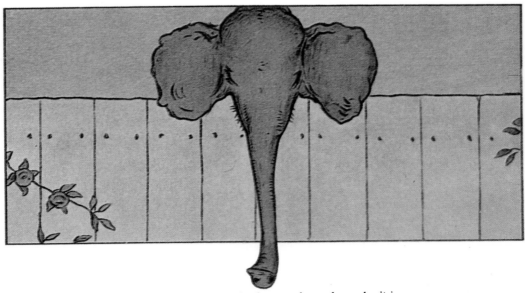

The Elephant leans on the fence and wonders why it is

And side by side, with eye-glass fixed, they strolled along the street.

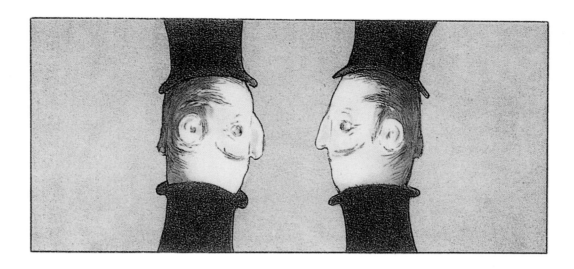

Two "chappies" on the avenue one foggy day did meet,

But when he comes to speak his piece just see what animation!

How quietly this learned Man writes out his great oration,

Probably the most ambitious approach to upside-down drawings as cartoons for children was undertaken by Gustave Verbeek. In 1903 and 1904, he published a cartoon series in the Sunday editions of the *New York Herald* called "The Upside Downs of Little Lady Lovekins and Old Man Muffaroo." He drew six panels, telling a story about his two main characters. He cleverly drew his two main characters, Little Lady Lovekins and Old Man Muffaroo, so that each becomes the other when the page is inverted. When the page is turned upside down, the story continues on with the same six panels! Clouds become bushes, and water becomes the sky. For two years, Verbeek drew more than sixty such stories!

Unlike the Sunday papers of today, where color cartoon strips are standard, Verbeek's work was printed in black and white. We take the liberty of presenting them in color—as they would be seen if Verbeek were active today—and modify some of his text to make it more appropriate for our time.

Note how he uses the simple inversion of a clock on the wall to indicate the passage of time in "A Night of Terror," and makes an early, if somewhat crude, attempt at ambigrams in two of the panels of "The Bad Snake and the Good Wizard." He also uses the visual perspective of objects in the distance appearing smaller than closer objects when he "shrinks" the elephant in "A Story of Narrow Escapes." In "The Fairy Palace," the "funny little fairies'" hair and headbands in frame 5 become the mouths of the bearded "loathsome hobgoblins" in frame 8. In addition, he uses the same drawing to show the two main characters entering the fairy palace in frame 1, then leaving in frame 12!

"A NIGHT OF TERROR"

2. At last Muffaroo consents, and they find it really very delightful outside. But they get a sort of creepy feeling, especially when they see a big, black form moving toward them.

11. At last she hears Muffaroo calling her in a whisper, and she drops to the ground and they both run to the house.

12. When they get home, the clock is pointing at twenty minutes to five, which shows that they have been out something over six hours. Yet in that short time, the four hairs on Muffaroo's head have turned white. MORAL: Little people should not go out late at night.

1. Lovekins and Muffaroo are sitting in the window-seat, looking out at the moon. It is ten minutes past ten, and rather late for little people to go out, but Lovekins wants to go.

3. A tall man with a large hooked nose leans over. "Muffaroo, there is a Squeedlejunk coming," says he, and then he vanishes like a ghost. All of this is very awful indeed.

10. Every now and then, some hideous beast passes under her.

9. Lovekins climbs up a tree, where she hangs for some time.

4. But now they hear a screech that sends Lovekins jumping up about ten feet in the air. Then there is a crunching and a snorting, and a pit-a-pat of heavy feet.

5. And along comes the worst-looking animal that they have ever seen.

8. And behind them comes still another horrible animal.

7. But Lovekins follows close at his heels.

6. Old Man Muffaroo is the first to find his legs.

"A STORY OF NARROW ESCAPES"

12. They catch him and carry him home, where he plays with them very nicely. He becomes very fond of his master and mistress, and, if you go to call on them, you may very well see the elephant curled up on Lady Lovekins's lap.

11. "After him," cries Lovekins. "You go one way and I'll go the other."

1. Lovekins and Muffaroo see an enormous elephant rolling on his back in the grass. They manage to steal away quietly before he sees them. That is narrow escape number one.

2. Later on, Lovekins picks up a curious bottle containing some strange liquid. "Don't drink it," says Muffaroo, but Lovekins touches a drop of liquid to her tongue.

10. Then Lovekins and Muffaroo have to run to keep him in sight, for he has jumped into the grass and scurried into the woods.

9. "Oh, isn't he going to be cute," she cries, as the elephant rolls around, getting smaller and smaller until it is about the size of a dog.

3. Instantly she feels herself growing smaller, but by vigorous spitting, she saves herself from losing more than one inch. That is narrow escape number two, and Muffaroo just groans.

4. Now this he should not have done, for the quick-eared elephant hears him and comes galloping up to see what is going on behind the trees. They are discovered! What is to be done?

8. "Come," says Lovekins, "let us watch him grow little."

7. "That will settle him," says Old Man Muffaroo. "We need not be afraid now."

5. Quick as a flash, Muffaroo hands the bottle to the elephant. The big fellow innocently sips the contents. He seems to like the stuff. That is narrow escape number three.

6. Lovekins and Muffaroo, peering out from the bushes, see him lie on his back in order to pour it down his throat more easily, for elephants cannot drink from bottles without lying on their backs.

12. And they both do a little dance to celebrate her deliverance.

11. Dragging the dead snake out of the way, Muffaroo now helps little Lady Lovekins out of her prison.

1. They come upon a curious old hollow tree one fine day. Old Man Muffaroo thinks he must really have a look inside.

2. So he gaily steps into the hold, when horrors!, he feels something soft and slimy and wriggly, and he jumps out again.

10. Then suddenly he remembers the Wizard's words, and loudly he cries out the dreaded name, at which the serpent promptly rolls over and dies.

9. There the snake awaits him, and a terrible fight takes place in which Muffaroo—at first—has the better of it. But in spite of his new strength, he finds himself slowly being drawn into the hole.

3. Out comes a big snake after him, but Muffaroo, shame on him, runs away, Leaving poor Lady Lovekins standing there. "How do you do?" she stammers, trying to push the snake away.

4. But the snake will not be pushed away. He wraps himself around her instead, and pulls her into the hollow tree, where he intends to keep her captive.

8. The magic liquor gives Muffaroo the strength of 100 men. "Have you seen the serpent?" he asks as he passes the squirrel again. "No serpent, sah," is the reply, and the Old Man goes to the tree.

7. The Wizard produces a bottle containing a magic liquor, which he gives to Muffaroo and says, "Fear not the serpent more! When you meet him, call forth the name of "Opnohop Moy" and he shall die.

5. Muffaroo, meanwhile, has been running, and now he crawls, his legs having given out. He asks a squirrel if the Wizard Opnohop Moy does not live a little further on. "Yes, furders on," replies the squirrel.

6. Now the great Wizard Opnohop Moy lives in a barrel, and all the animals and reptiles fear him. Muffaroo arrives at his place and tells him the sad tale of little Lady Lovekins's imprisonment.

"THE FAIRY PALACE"

12. Then they climb down, more frightened than hurt, and run away, and Lovekins resolves never to give way to idle curiosity again.

11. He tosses them right through the door, into the branches of a palm tree outside.

1. One day Lovekins and Muffaroo come to a beautiful lake, just like a mirror. On the shore they see a lovely palace toward which they make their way.

2. "Let us go in!" cried little Lady Lovekins. Since the big door stands wide open, in they go.

10. Then a huge bull comes rushing out at them and tosses them with his horns.

9. The hobgoblins all at once slip back into their closet, because a terrible roaring now fills the whole palace. Lovekins and Muffaroo tremble.

3. Inside, a great genie floats up to them in a cloud of smoke. "You will find two mysterious closets," he says. "The one on the right you may open, but the left-hand one, open not! Oh, open not!"

4. Then he vanishes. Pretty soon they find the two mysterious closets. Muffaroo remembers the genie's words.

8. Instantly a hoard of loathsome hobgoblins come trooping out, and taking hold of our little heroes, they maul them and throw them up in the air.

7. But when his back is turned, Lovekins quietly goes to the forbidden door on the left-hand side and opens it just enough for a tiny peek.

5. So he opens only the right-hand door, and behold! Out come a lot of funny little fairies, singing sweet songs to them.

6. The fairies go back, and Muffaroo closes the door again. "I wonder what is in the other closet," says Lovekins. "And that we shall never know!" replies Old Man Muffaroo.

CHAPTER 6

A SLIGHT TURN

In this chapter, you don't turn the book upside down to see the second image, but you do have to turn it ninety degrees to the left or right.

As we did in "Upside Down," we will start with ambigrams. However, in this case, you do not see the same word when it is turned. You see a translation from Chinese to English. These are bilingual ambigrams by David Moser, who calls them "dual-reading calligraphs." Moser began his work on such images as a graduate student at Indiana University, and is currently a translator living in Beijing.

The first example, if turned counterclockwise, can easily be read as "England," and that is exactly what it says in Chinese when it is held upright. The second figure has to be turned clockwise to read "China," but that is what it says in Chinese when you first look at it.

The third figure, when turned clockwise, becomes "Tokyo," and the fourth becomes "America" when turned counterclockwise. Moser does not limit his work to geographical locations, but we have chosen these few as examples.

Obviously—with these and other ambigrams—most of the letters do not look like ones we are used to seeing. This is just another example of the flexibility of

Reprinted by permission, Center for Research on Concepts and Cognition, Indiana University, Bloomington.

the human mind. This flexibility is basically what *Seeing Double* is all about. The artists have shown this flexibility in their creations, and we show flexibility in our interpretation. We do this all of the time. While *Seeing Double* is about two or more images in one, if we think of the vast number of ways a letter in the alphabet can be presented visually to us without eliciting any confusion, we have additional testimony to the flexibility of the human mind. Thus, departing from the thrust of this book, look at the array of visual images, all of which are immediately interpreted as the letter "A," and it makes no difference if we see an uppercase or lowercase version.

It is fascinating that even with all these different visual stimuli, we see all of them as the letter "A." Yet if you make the very minor visual change of attaching a short vertical line to either side of what is basically an "o," the shift from a lowercase "d" to a "b" is detected immediately and the two are distinctly different letters! Here, a minor visual change is perceived as a major conceptual one.

Reprinted by permission, Center for Research on Concepts and Cognition, Indiana University, Bloomington.

The next figure is an eighteenth-century drawing by an unknown artist. The drawing is called "The Hidden Giant." He can be seen when the figure is turned counterclockwise.

From The Paradox Box, *Redstone Press, 1993.*

In the next figure, the frog becomes a horse when turned counterclockwise.

From the collection of Keith Kay.

Next we see the face of a clown, but it becomes the whole circus when turned clockwise (Kettelkamp, 1974).

The final figures in this chapter are all by American graphic artist Paul Agule. We saw other examples of his work in "Ambiguous Figures." In the first, a woman's face is transformed into a cat looking at figures, which could be worms, when turned counterclockwise. Finally, when turned clockwise, the mountain goat seated on the side of a hill becomes a bird sitting on some branches!

a seated cat observing some objects.

Paul Agule

A demure oriental lady or...

Paul Agule

A bird sitting in the branches. (the beak was previously the goat's horns)

A mountain goat on the side of a hill

CHAPTER 7

TILTING, MOVING, AND GETTING UP CLOSE

In this chapter, you will have to move the book in different ways to see the second image. For the first few, you must hold the book at eye level and tilt it away from you. In many cases, we have placed an arrow to show you where you should look.

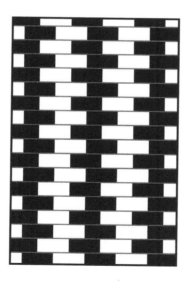

In the first four figures, lines that appear to be slightly bowed can be seen as perfectly straight and parallel when held at eye level and tilted away. The backgrounds on which they have been printed tend to draw your eye either inward or outward.

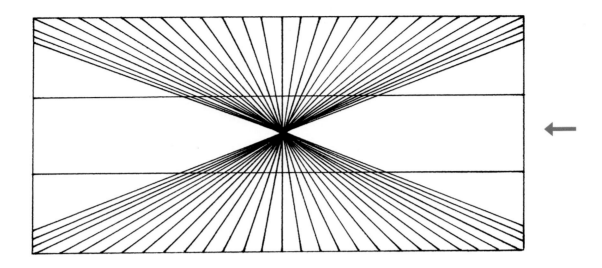

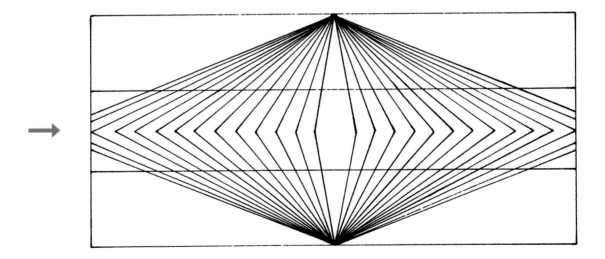

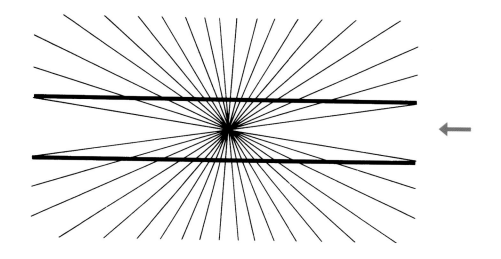

In the next figure, the small crossing lines also draw the eye away from seeing that all of the longer lines run parallel to each other.

Two quite strong distortions of straight lines can be seen in the next two figures. The first is popularly known as "The Cafe Wall Illusion." The staggered brick images seem to make the spaces between the levels of brick curve slightly, but you can see the bricks have been perfectly laid when you tilt the image away from you at eye level.

In the next figure, the blocks have been put on top of one another to make a colorful wall. However, they don't look too steady. It looks as if each one has been placed unevenly on top of the one below it. It may not look steady, but the bricklayer did the job perfectly. You

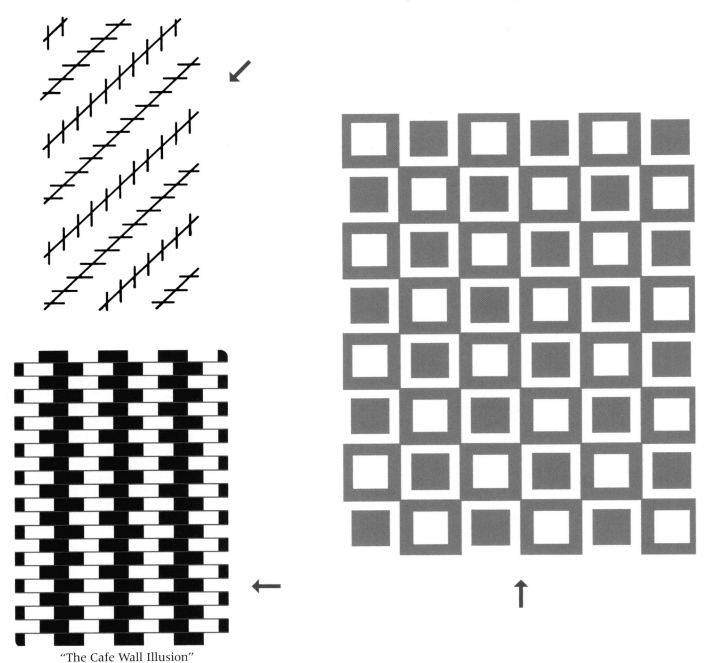

"The Cafe Wall Illusion"

can see this if you hold the book at eye level and tilt the page away from you, closing one eye.

The next three figures can be seen as three-dimensional if they are viewed a certain way at eye level. In the first, all of the lines have been drawn from a point of origin off the page on your lower right. Turn the book so that the arrow is your point of origin and tip it away from you. Close one eye and look at the figure. The lines should appear to be standing straight out from the paper! This illusion was first presented by the well-known psychologist William James (James, 1908).

The same principle was applied in the pen and wash drawing on the right. It was done in 1870 by J.W. Schwenck and is called "A Castle." The castle seems to stand up straight when you view it with one eye and tilt the book away from you.

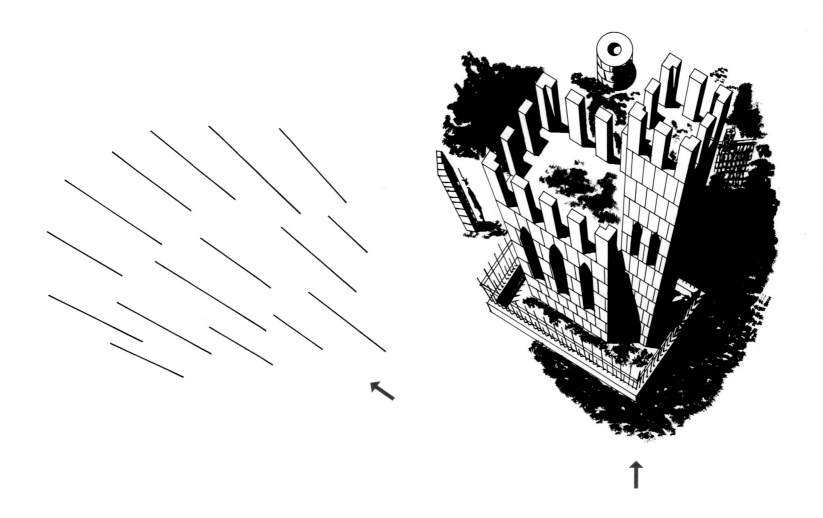

The final illustration that requires you to tilt the book away was first reported, once again, by William James in his classic 1908 text, *Principles of Psychology.* The figure is simply two crossed lines. However, you can "create" a third line at their intersection. It looks like a short pin sticking up through the paper! Hold the book so that the cross point is directly in front of you. If you cross your eyes slightly, you will see a third line that isn't there. The images from each of the long lines fuse to form the third (illusory) line (James, 1908).

To see a different image in the next two figures, you have to hold the book very close to your eyes. In the first figure, the squares look perfectly normal and simply centered in the circle. However, when viewed with one eye at about a distance of an inch, the figure seems to bulge out at you. Exactly the opposite happens with the second figure. As printed on the page, the "squares" do not look square. The figure seems to be somewhat concave. Viewed with one eye at a distance of just a few inches, the squares become much more regular and the figure looks flatter than it did.

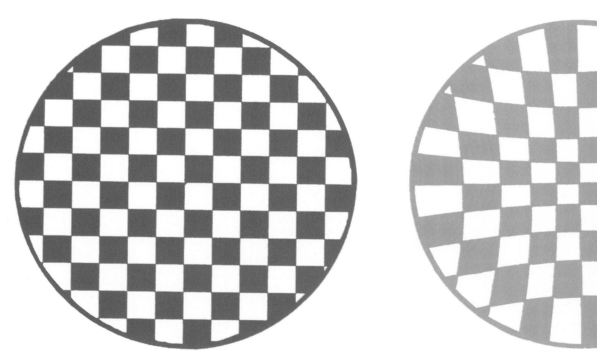

The final figure in this chapter looks something like a target, with concentric circles and a solid circle in the center. In this case, to see the second image you must move the book with a slight circular motion. When you do so, spoke-like images appear within the figure. We suggest you make a photocopy of this figure. If you do, and you rotate the copy slowly while holding it near the stationary book, both will appear to have spokes: the one you are moving, and the one that is stationary!

CHAPTER 8

OTHER WAYS OF SEEING DOUBLE

In this chapter we will briefly explore a variety of means of seeing more than one image in a single figure.

In "Hermann's Grid," when you look at the intersections between the purple squares, there appear to be small light purple spots. Similarly, there are light spots at the purple intersections when the color of the squares is reversed. However, if you look directly at any single intersection, the spot disappears. The same is true for the dark lines separating the white squares in the other figure. It has been found that the more intersections you have, the stronger the effect becomes. In addition, the regularity of the spaces between the squares plays a role in the strength of this phenomenon. It may seem a bit of a stretch to include this image in *Seeing Double,* but the fact is that if you want to see a gray spot at an intersection—you cannot look at it!

A completely different visual phenomenon involving a double image is called a "negative aftereffect." Negative aftereffects occur when the light sensitive receptors in your eyes—the rods and cones—become fatigued when there is prolonged or strong stimulation. Thus, we often see a dark dot after our picture is taken

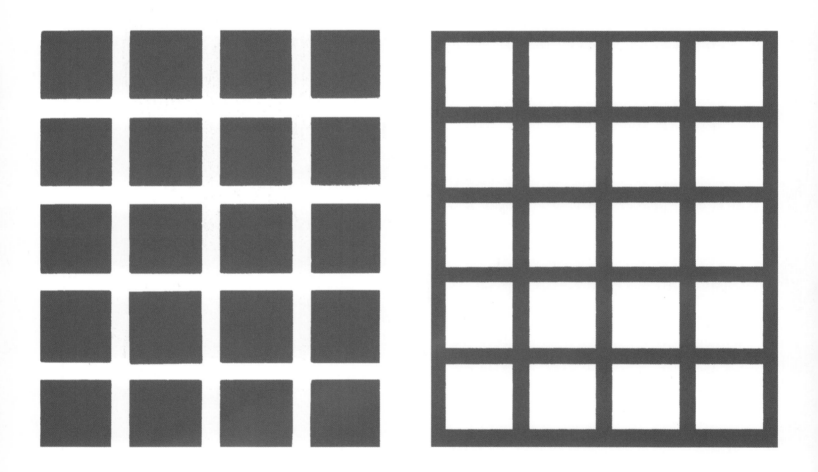

with a flash bulb. The neutral light that enters the eye after the prolonged or strong stimulation does not stimulate these receptors effectively, and the opposite effect is seen. Since we cannot present strong stimuli to your eye in a book, to see the negative aftereffect you must stare at the figure for 30 seconds or more under a bright light.

Our first two examples of negative aftereffects are presented to you in black. The negative effect comes from the fact that the opposite of black is white. The first example appears to be a black light bulb with a white filament. If you stare at it for 30 seconds or so, and then look at the blank area to its left, the bulb seems to light! In fact, it is seen as a somewhat brighter white than the surface you are looking at. Thus, you see a black light at one time and a white light at another. The effect will not last long since the visual stimulus of staring for about 30 seconds is not that strong. Sometimes you can prolong the effect a bit by blinking your eyes (Block and Yuker, 1989).

There are some interesting characteristics of negative aftereffects. In addition to the white light appearing to be whiter than the surface you look at, you can "project" the image and make it appear larger. If instead of looking at a blank sheet of paper, which is close to you, you shifted your gaze to a white wall some distance away, the bulb would appear much larger. In addition, you can prove that it is the cell structure of your eye that retains the image, since if you tilt your head, the image is tilted, but not the surface at which you are looking.

Our second black-and-white figure that produces an aftereffect becomes the face of Jesus Christ after you have stared at it for 30 seconds or so.

Negative aftereffects also work in color. Just as black and white are visual opposites, colors have their opposites as well. These are called "complementary colors." An afterimage of a color will be seen as that color's complement.

We see color (and black and white) because our eyes are able to receive a certain range of electromagnetic wavelengths. This kind of energy travels in waves that vary greatly in length. Some, called gamma waves, measure only about 4 ten-trillionths of an inch! Some are over 18 miles long! These are the electromagnetic waves used for transoceanic broadcasts. In between there are X rays, infrared rays, short wave and regular

broadcast radio signals. The visual spectrum to which our eyes respond consists of relatively short electromagnetic waves ranging from 16 millionths of an inch to about 32 millionths of an inch in length.

The colors we see all have slightly different wavelengths from each other. If we take the spectrum, which can be thought of as a straight line of increasing wavelengths, and bend it around in a circle so that the shortest waves touch the longest waves, we create a "color wheel." Colors that are opposite each other on the wheel are complementary colors. Thus, on the color wheel we would find that red is opposite blue-green, and blue is opposite orange. When we create a negative afterimage from a strong or prolonged stimulus, the afterimage is the complementary or opposite color.

We have added a bit of color to the next figure, called "Marilyn's Lips." If you stare at her lips for about 60 seconds and then look at the white space on the left, you can see her wearing red lipstick and a red dress. Again, the reverse figure does not last long, although blinking may help to retain it.

The next figures in this chapter all appear to be strange looking flags. However, if you stare at each of them to produce a negative afterimage, as the cones of your eyes become fatigued when neutral light then stimulates them, you will perceive the opposite colors and identify the flags. The yellow, green, and black become the familiar red, white, and blue of the flags of the United States and the United Kingdom. The green circle on the black background becomes the flag of Japan, and the same principle applies to the German flag. You can use the bottom of the page to see the afterimages.

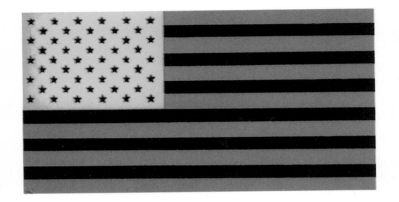

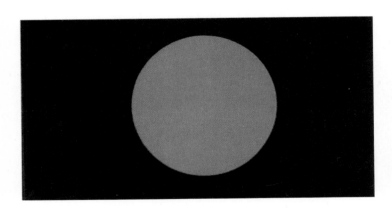

However, under certain conditions, staring at an image can make it disappear. We can see this in the "fading dot" illusion. To demonstrate this, hold the book at arm's length or step away a short distance. Stare at the blue dot in the middle of the circle for about a minute or so without moving your eyes or your head. The dot will gradually fade into the green area. As soon as you move your eyes or your head, the blue dot will reappear. Although you are not aware of it, your eyes are constantly making small movements even when you attempt to hold them steady. You are therefore constantly getting minor amounts of new information, even if you are attempting to look only at the blue dot. Because the dot does not have a distinct edge, the green area gradually covers the blue in your eye—since it is so much larger and has a defined area—and the dot disappears. This illusion was developed by Cija Briegleb and Zach Waller while they were students at San Francisco State University in 1994.

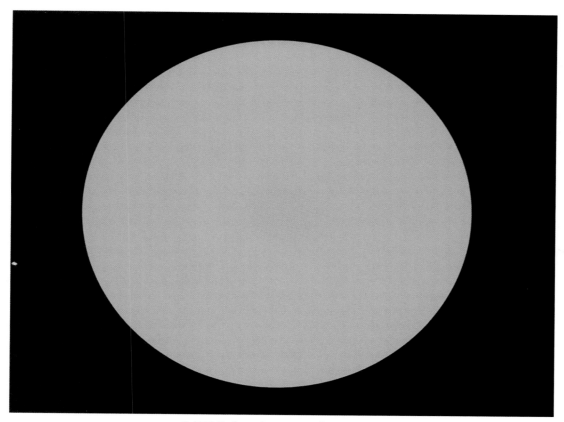

© 2001 Exploratorium. www.exploratorium.edu

The reverse of this is true for "The Woman with the Amazing Eyes." In this case, if you stare at her eyes, which appear to be closed, you seem to see her open them! Her eyelids are quite small, and her eyebrows and lashes are much darker. As your eyes make these tiny movements, the lighter, smaller areas of the lids are replaced with the larger, darker brows and lashes. This figure first appeared in 1910 as a promotional postcard for *Answers*, a popular family weekly magazine in the United Kingdom.

From The Paradox Box, *Redstone Press, 1993.*

For the final image in this chapter, we return to one of Scott Kim's ambigrams. In this case, you will need outside help to see the second image. This time we won't tell you what the second image is. To see it, turn to the backside of this page, and hold it up to a bright light so that the image shows through the paper. Then turn the book upside down. Or, you can also see the second image by turning the book upside down and looking at it reflected in a mirror. In a very real sense, it is a reflection of one of the major goals in writing this book.

© Scott Kim.

There is often more than one way of looking at something—
visually and mentally!

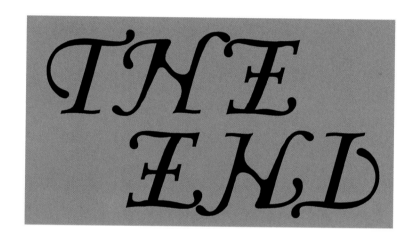

There is often more than one way of looking at something—
visually and mentally!

REFERENCES

Block, J.R. and Yuker, H.E. (1989). *Can You Believe Your Eyes?* Bruner/Mazel Publishers, New York.

Botwinick, J. (1961). Husband and Father-in-law: A reversible figure. *American Journal of Psychology*, 74, 312–313.

Bradley, D.R. and Dumais, S.R. (1975). Ambiguous cognitive contours. *Nature,* 257, 582–584.

Calder, J.R. (1993). *The Amazing Topsy-Turvy Storybook.* J.R. Calder, 52 Ulster Crescent, Edinburgh, Scotland, EH8 7JL.

Draper, S.W. (1978). The Penrose triangle and a family of related figures. *Perception,* 7, 283–296. Pion, London.

Fisher, G.H. (1967a). Measuring Ambiguity. *American Journal of Psychology*, 80, 541–557.

Fisher, G.H. (1967b). Preparation of ambiguous stimulus materials. *Perception and Psychophysics*, 4, 189–192.

Fisher, G.H. (1968a). Ambiguity of form: Old and new. *Perception and Psychophysics*, 4, 189–192.

Fisher, G.H. (1968b). Mother, father and daughter: A three-aspect ambiguous figure. *American Journal of Psychology*, 81, 274–277.

Gardner, M. (1970). Of optical illusions from figures that are undetectable to hot dogs that float. *Scientific American*, 222, May, 124–127.

Hill, W.E. (1915). My wife and my mother-in-law. *Puck,* November 6th, 11.

Huffman, D.A. (1971). Impossible Objects as Nonsense Sentences. In *Machine Intelligence* 6 Eds., B. Meltzer, D. Michie. Edinburgh University Press, Edinburgh. 295–323.

James, W. (1908). *Principles of Psychology, Volume II.* Henry Holt, New York.

Kay, K. (1988). *Take a Closer Look!* Bright Intervals Books, Bolton, England.

Kay, K. (1997). *The Little Giant Book of Optical Illusions.* Sterling Publishing Co., New York.

Kettelkamp, L. (1974). *Tricks of the Mind: The Story of Optical Illusions.* William Morrow & Co., New York.

Kim, S. (1989). *Inversions.* W.H. Freeman & Co., New York.

Langdon, J. (1992). *Wordplay: Ambigrams and Reflections on the Art of Ambigrams.* Harcourt, Brace, Jovanovich Publishers, New York.

Miller, J. *The Paradox Box.* Redstone Press, London, England.

Moser, D. (1990). *Chinese-English Ambigrams,* CRCC Report #45.

Newell, P. (1902a). *Topsys & Turvys.* Dover Publications Inc., New York.

Newell P. (1902b). *Topsys & Turvys.* Charles E. Tuttle Co., Rutland, Vermont.

Redstone Press (1998).*Upside-Down Head.* London, England.

Rock, I., Hall, S., and Davis, J. (1994). Why do ambiguous figures reverse? *Acta Psychologica,* 87, 33–59.

Rothenstein, J. and Gooding, M. (1999). *The Playful Eye.* Chronicle Books, San Francisco.

Schuster, D.H. (1964). A new ambiguous figure: A three-stick clevis. *American Journal of Psychology,* 77, 673.

Whistler, R. and Whistler, L. (1978). *AHA.* John Murray Publishers Ltd., London, England.

NAME AND TERM INDEX

IMAGE INDEX